COUNTRIES IN OUR WORLD

 # ITALY

Ann Weil

W

FRANKLIN WATTS
LONDON • SYDNEY

This edition 2012

First published in 2010 by
Franklin Watts
338 Euston Road
London NW1 3BH

Franklin Watts Australia
Level 17/207 Kent Street
Sydney NSW 2000

Produced for Franklin Watts by
White-Thomson Publishing Ltd
+44 (0) 845 362 8240
www.wtpub.co.uk

Series consultant: Rob Bowden
Editor: Sonya Newland
Designer: Clare Nicholas
Picture researcher: Amy Sparks

A CIP catalogue record for this book is available
from the British Library.

Dewey Classification: 945'.093

ISBN 978 1 4451 0807 0

Printed in Malaysia

Franklin Watts is a division of Hachette Children's
Books, an Hachette UK company.

www.hachette.co.uk

Contents

Introducing Italy

Italy is one of the most developed countries in the world. It is a popular tourist destination and is famous for its fashion and its food. Although it is a relatively small country, its capital Rome was once the centre of a huge empire.

BASIC DATA

Official name: Italian Republic

Capital: Rome

Size: 301,230 sq km (116,306 sq miles)

Population: 61,016,804

Currency: Euro

Where in the world?

The boot-shaped Italian peninsula in southern Europe stretches 800 km (500 miles) southwards into the Mediterranean. The Alps mountain range forms a natural boundary with France, Switzerland, Austria and Slovenia in the north. The rest of the country is surrounded by sea, and Italy has thousands of kilometres of coastline. Italy also includes Sicily, Sardinia and several smaller islands.

▶ *Italy has land borders with Austria, France, Slovenia and Switzerland, as well as the two small countries of San Marino and Vatican City.*

Ancient civilization

This modern, developed country has a long history. The Roman civilization began in around the tenth century BCE, and the ancient Romans are remembered for their development of law, art and language. This civilization gradually spread, and by the first century CE, a vast Roman Empire stretched right across Europe, North Africa and the Near East. The Roman Empire lasted until the fifth century.

▼ *The Trevi Fountain is one of many famous landmarks in Rome, the ancient capital of the huge Roman Empire.*

IT'S A FACT!

Two of the world's smallest countries lie completely within Italy's borders. Vatican City (or the Holy See) in Rome is the smallest country in the world, at only 0.5 sq km (0.2 sq miles). San Marino, on Mount Titano in north-central Italy, is 52 sq km (24 sq miles), and is the world's fifth smallest country.

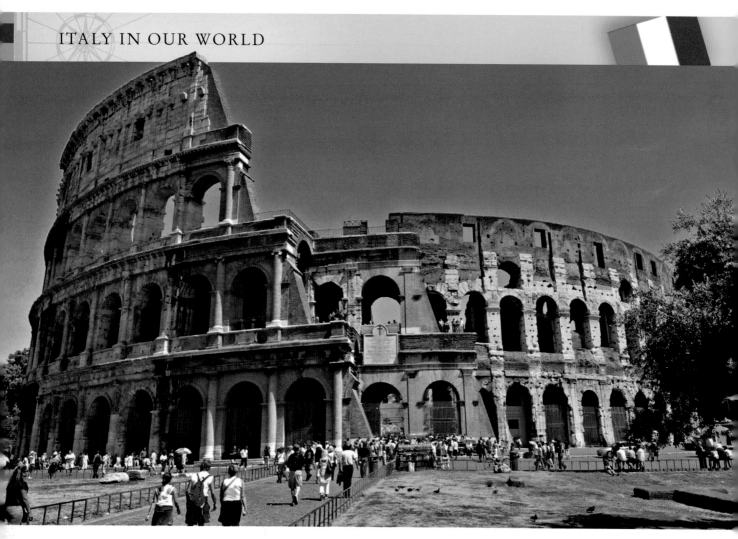

Roman remains

Remains of the Roman civilization can still be seen in all parts of the former empire, and the technology the ancient Romans developed continues to influence our modern world. The Romans also built many great public buildings, including the famous Colosseum in Rome, where gladiators battled each other to the death.

City-states

After the fall of the Roman Empire, some cities in Italy became powerful independent states known as city-states. These were independently ruled, and each area

▲ *Work began on the Colosseum in Rome in 70 CE, and it was completed 10 years later. Over the centuries, earthquakes have damaged the remains.*

developed its own sense of identity. Places such as Venice, Florence and Milan grew rich from trade with countries in Europe and Asia.

The Kingdom of Italy

Between the fifteenth and the nineteenth centuries, France, Spain and Austria all invaded Italy and took control of different regions. Eventually the Italians won the fight against their foreign rulers, and the country was united as the Kingdom of Italy in 1861.

IT STARTED HERE

The Renaissance

After the fall of the Roman Empire in the fifth century, much of the Romans' knowledge was lost or forgotten. In the fourteenth century, however, people became interested in learning and the arts once again. This period in history became known as the Renaissance, which means 'rebirth'. It began in Italy and spread throughout Europe. Art, music, literature and learning all flourished during the Renaissance.

The sweet life

After World War II (1939–45), Italy became a republic rather than a kingdom. It recovered more quickly from the effects of the war than many other European countries. The economy boomed and Italians enjoyed high incomes and a relaxed lifestyle known as *la dolce vita* ('the sweet life'). However, the global economic crisis that began in 2008 hit Italy harder than many other countries. This was partly because the Italian economy relied on manufacturing and exporting products, and when the crisis hit, other countries stopped buying so many Italian-made goods. A survey found that Italians were the least happy people in Western Europe.

THE HOME OF...

Coffee culture

Coffee was 'discovered' by Europeans around 1600, when the first shipment of coffee from the Muslim world arrived in the port city of Venice, Italy. From Italy, the fashion for drinking coffee spread throughout Europe. Today, you can order an *espresso* almost anywhere in the world. This strong-tasting coffee is made using a machine invented in Italy.

Landscapes and environment

Most of Italy's landscape is rugged and mountainous, but there are some flat plain areas, and long stretches of sandy beach along the coastline. The country is also dotted with lakes and volcanoes.

Coast and mountains

Surrounded on three sides by the Mediterranean Sea, Italy's total coastline – including the large islands of Sicily and Sardinia – is 7,600 km (4,722 miles). In the north, the Alps separate Italy from the rest of Europe, and the Apennine Mountains run from the Alps in the north to the toe of the boot in the south, forming a kind of backbone through the country. This rugged mountain range includes Europe's southernmost glacier, the Calderone. Northern Italy has hot summers and cold winters. Southern Italy has even hotter summers, and winters there are usually mild and rainy.

GLOBAL LEADER

World Heritage Sites
Italy has 47 World Heritage Sites – places considered to be of special cultural significance – more than any other country in the world. These range from royal palaces and cathedrals to lakes, valleys and prehistoric remains.

▼ *The island of Sardinia, famous for its beautiful beaches, lies off the west coast of Italy.*

Volcanoes

Italy is home to three very active volcanoes, which have all erupted in the last 100 years. Mount Vesuvius, in south-west Italy, is the only active volcano in mainland Europe. Mount Etna is on the island of Sicily and is almost constantly erupting. The Stromboli volcano, on an island of the same name, has been erupting almost continually since 1932. It releases lava and emissions of gas and ash.

Wildlife

Despite Italy's relatively small size, more than one-third of all European animal species can be found there. Many native animals are under threat, but efforts are being made to protect them and increase their numbers again. Some endangered animals can be found in national parks and in the dense forests in the Abruzzo region of the Apennines. A national park not far from

▲ *The ancient city of Pompeii, buried under rock and ash after Vesuvius (in the background) erupted, has now been excavated.*

IT'S A FACT!

One of the most famous volcanic disasters in history occurred in Italy in 79 CE when Vesuvius erupted. Burning ash and volcanic rock rained down on the ancient city of Pompeii. People suffocated under clouds of poisonous gases, and the entire city remained buried – and mostly forgotten – for more than 1,500 years.

Rome is home to a handful of formerly endangered species: the Apennine wolf, Marsican bear, fox, mountain goat and Apennine lynx.

Earthquakes

Because Italy lies on two fault lines – large cracks in the rock on the Earth's surface – it has suffered from many earthquakes over the centuries. In April 2009, a huge earthquake hit the thirteenth-century mountain city of L'Aquila, in the Abruzzo region. When the earthquake struck, the old buildings crumbled and the whole city was destroyed. Almost 300 people were killed and 68,000 more were left homeless.

Melting the Alps

Like most other countries, Italy faces a number of environmental issues. One of the most serious is the effect that global warming is having on the landscape. As temperatures rise, warmer-than-usual weather has caused glaciers to melt in the Alps on Italy's border with Switzerland. The landscape has changed so much that in 2009, Italy and Switzerland agreed to change the position of the border between the two countries.

▲ *The 2009 earthquake in the Abruzzo region was the worst to hit Italy in 30 years.*

Flooding in Venice

Another effect of global warming has been an increase in floods. Flooding has always been a problem in the Italian city of Venice, which is made up of more than 100 small islands in a marshy lagoon. Recently the floods have been much worse, though, damaging many old buildings and the precious artefacts housed there. The Venice Barrier is being built to prevent water from entering the lagoon during very high tides.

PLACE IN THE WORLD

Total area: **301,230 sq km (116,306 sq miles)**

Percentage of world land area: **0.2%**

World ranking: **71st**

Pollution

Pollution is another major environmental issue in Italy, as polluting gases are released into the atmosphere by factories in the big cities. In 2006, a new way to fight pollution was introduced in several Italian cities: special pavement bricks. When exposed to light, a chemical in the bricks reacts with the poisonous gas carbon monoxide in the air, turning it into water and carbon dioxide.

▼ *Heavy traffic – like this in Naples – is also contributing to air pollution in Italy.*

IT'S A FACT!

Italy is planning to reduce pollution further by encouraging people to hire environmentally friendly electric cars. As part of this 'e-mobility' plan, more than 100 electric cars were made available in Rome, Milan and Pisa in 2010, with special stations where they can be 'charged' – the electric equivalent of petrol stations.

Population and migration

About 94 per cent of Italy's population is ethnic Italian, and the country has far fewer ethnic minorities than its neighbours in Europe. There are only a few small minority groups that speak languages other than Italian.

Where do Italians live?

Italy has a population of just over 61 million, two-thirds of whom live in cities. In fact, Italy has the fifth highest population density in Europe. Most of the industry is found in the north of the country, and this is more populated than the south as people go there in search of work. The southern part of the country, including the large island of Sicily, is more rural. The people there also tend to be poorer than those in northern Italy.

PLACE IN THE WORLD

Population: **61,016,804**

Percentage of world total: **0.9%**

World ranking: **23rd**

▼ *Italy has an ageing population. Here, elderly men gather to pass the time discussing business and politics.*

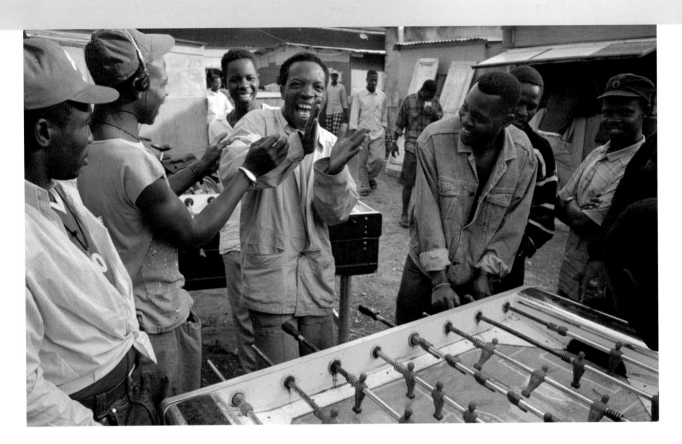

Immigrants in Italy

Around 4.2 million immigrants live in Italy. Around a quarter of them come from other parts of Europe, particularly Eastern Europe, but there are also many from North Africa and Asia. In some countries immigrants have been accepted by the native people, but in Italy immigrants often live in separate communities that keep their own customs and traditions rather than adopting Italian culture. Some Italians are more suspicious of immigrants than other Europeans, and feel that they have too many rights. Most immigrants have settled in northern Italy, where there are more jobs, and the fear and dislike of immigrants by Italians is stronger here than in other parts of the country.

▲ *Villa Literno, near Naples, was once a summer resort. Now, immigrants from Africa live in the old, run-down holiday apartments.*

Illegal immigration

Although many immigrants to Italy go through the proper channels and settle there legally, many more arrive in the country illegally. This is easier to do than in some other countries, because the long coastline means it is readily accessible by boat, and immigrants may be able to arrive undetected by the authorities. Many illegal immigrants come from south-east Europe and Africa in search of jobs and a better quality of life than they have in their own countries.

Emigration

Southern Italy has a long history of emigration and there are now as many people with Italian heritage living outside Italy as there are in the country itself – about 60 million. From the 1870s to the 1970s, about 25 million Italians left Italy. Most were men – farmers from southern Italy and the island of Sicily. They left home hoping to find work elsewhere.

IT'S A FACT!

America was named after the fifteenth-century Italian explorer Amerigo Vespucci, who made several voyages to the Americas, and other parts of the world.

Italian-Americans

The USA was one of the most popular destinations for Italians looking for a new life. They could make more money working in American cities and factories than they could at home. Although some stayed in the USA, millions took their new wealth home to their families in Italy. Today, about six per cent of people identify themselves as Italian-Americans, and Italian-Americans form the fourth largest ethnic group in the USA.

▼ *A brass band at the Feast of San Gennaro, an Italian festival celebrated in the area known as Little Italy in New York, USA.*

FAMOUS ITALIAN

Lee Iacocca
(b. 1924)

The son of Italian immigrants, Iacocca became one of the most famous businessmen in the world. As president of Ford Motor Company and the chairman of Chrysler Corporation, he changed the way cars were built and sold in America. He also wrote several books about his experiences that continue to inspire business people today.

Life in a new country

There are now five million Italians living abroad. About half live in other countries of the European Union and the rest have settled mainly in the USA, South America and Australia. Most migrants, then as now, are from the poorer south. Italian immigrants to Western Europe, North and South America, and Australia tend to adapt well to life in a new country. They are usually proud of their Italian heritage, but still adopt some of the customs and traditions of their new country. Some have become successful business people, film and television stars or politicians.

▲ Lee Iacocca's parents left Italy in the 1920s and settled in the USA. He is now one of America's most famous businessmen.

Culture and lifestyles

Italian culture spread around the world during the time of the Roman Empire, and it continues to have a global influence today. Within Italy many traditions remain strong, but new ideas are coming in from other parts of the world at a faster rate than ever before.

Food

Pasta is Italy's national dish, and there are more than 100 different types. Pasta is usually served with sauces made from meat, vegetables or cheese. Another national dish, pizza, was invented by a cook in Naples in 1775, and is now one of the most popular foods in the world. While people in many other countries are relying more on fast food, however, Italians do not want to eat and run. Enjoying meals with family and friends is part of their way of life. The Slow Food Movement began in Italy as a reaction against this trend to eat on the go. Now, it encourages food appreciation in more than 80 countries.

IT'S A FACT!

Italian families save more money than the Japanese and Germans, and three times more than Americans.

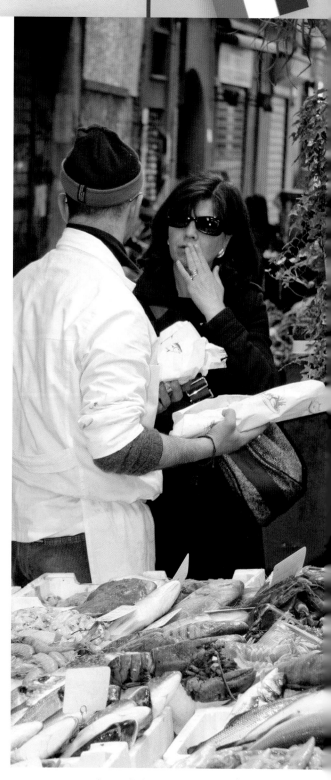

▲ *A woman buys fish at a market. Because of its long coastline, fresh fish is readily available in Italy.*

Family

Italians were once known for having large families, but now Italy has one of the lowest birth rates in Europe. Italians tend to live at home longer than people in other countries – unmarried children often live with their parents into their thirties. More than 80 per cent of Italian men aged between 18 and 30 still live with their parents. The average Italian man is 33 when his first child is born, making Italian men the oldest first-time fathers in Europe.

THE HOME OF...

Bologna University

The University of Bologna, in northern Italy, is the oldest continually operating university in Europe. It was founded in 1088 and continues to enrol both Italian and international students. It is Italy's top university and is particularly well known for its teaching of law.

Religion

The majority of Italians (90 per cent) are Catholic, and Italy has been an important centre for the Roman Catholic Church for more than 1,000 years. Today, this is the world's largest Christian Church, with one billion followers worldwide. The Catholic Church's base is in Vatican City, a tiny independent state surrounded by the city of Rome.

▼ *Pope Benedict XVI, leader of the Catholic Church, outside the Vatican in Rome.*

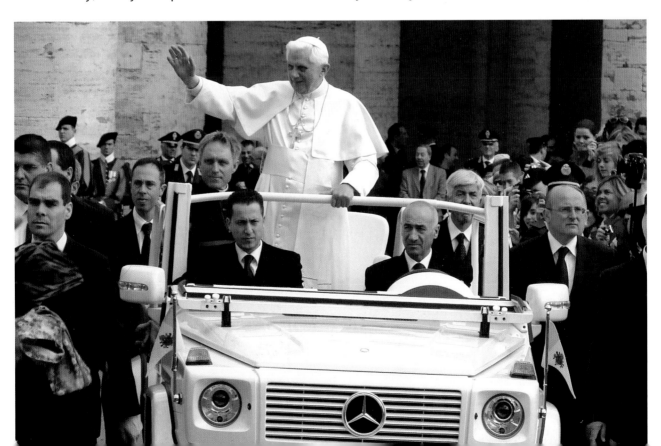

Italian music

Music has been an important part of Italian culture since ancient times. The viol, violin, cello and piano were all invented by Italians, and some of the world's most famous classical composers were Italian, including Giuseppe Verdi, Giacomo Puccini and Antonio Vivaldi. Opera singers such as Luciano Pavarotti and Andrea Bocelli have a worldwide following today. Although there are Italian pop stars, such as Eros Ramazzotti, young Italians also enjoy British and American pop music, as well as music from other European countries.

▼ *Italy is considered the birthplace of opera, and La Scala in Milan is one of the most famous opera houses in the world.*

FAMOUS ITALIAN

Luciano Pavarotti (1935–2007)

Opera star Luciano Pavarotti was born to a poor family in northern Italy. He became a huge celebrity, known for his size as well as his talent. His millions of fans included many young people who did not even like opera, after they saw him performing with rock stars such as Elton John, Sting and Bono.

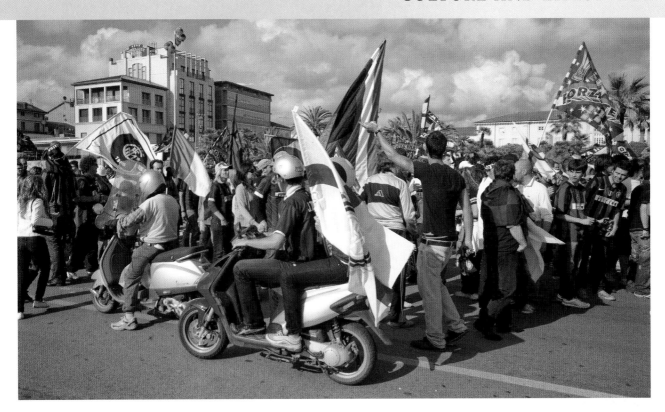

Football crazy

Italians are passionate about sport, especially football. Around five million Italians play football regularly and there are thousands of football clubs throughout the country. The Italian national team has won the World Cup four times – most recently in 2006 – more than any other country apart from Brazil. Many of the world's best footballers choose to play with Italian clubs, particularly the two most successful – Juventus and Milan. Italy also exports football stars to other countries.

▲ Fans of the football team AC Milan celebrate in the street. Most Italians are ardent football supporters.

The Olympics

Italian cities have hosted the Olympics three times – the 1956 Winter Olympics in Cortina d'Ampezzo, the 1960 Summer Olympics in Rome and the 2006 Winter Olympics in Turin, at which the Italian team won five gold medals and six bronze.

GLOBAL LEADER

Motor racing

Ferrari is probably the best-known racing team in the world, and the oldest and most successful team in Formula One. Since it was established in 1948, the Ferrari team has won 16 Constructors' Championships and 15 Drivers' Championships.

Economy and trade

In the second half of the twentieth century, Italy had one of the strongest economies in the world, but when the global economic crisis struck in the early 2000s, Italy was hit hard. It struggled to keep up with other countries in the EU and to compete in world markets.

Economic boom

Throughout the twentieth century, the Italian economy had its ups and downs. During World War II Italy fought alongside Germany, and when they lost the war many people feared that the Italian economy would take years to recover. However, a shift in focus from farming to industry helped the Italian economy survive the hardship experienced in many other countries after the war. By 1987, the economy was as strong as that of the UK.

Economic decline

As rapidly developing countries such as China and India became more industrialized in the early years of the twenty-first century, many Western nations found they could not compete with the low prices offered for products made in these countries. The economies of several Western nations, including Italy, began to decline.

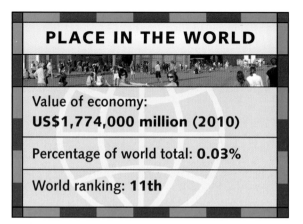

PLACE IN THE WORLD

Value of economy:
US$1,774,000 million (2010)

Percentage of world total: **0.03%**

World ranking: **11th**

◀ *High unemployment in Italy resulted in many people setting up street stalls to earn a living.*

In 2007, living standards in Italy fell behind those in Spain. Unemployment began to be a problem. In addition, Italy has a very high level of government debt, which led to a crisis in 2011 as the government struggled to borrow enough money to service this debt. Tough government spending cuts followed.

Farming

Only a quarter of Italy's land is suitable for farming, but this industry is still one of the most important in the country. It is famous for its wine and olive oil in particular, but in this area, too, Italy was overtaken by other countries in the 2000s. In 2008, a large Spanish food company bought the Italian company Bertolli, one of the world's best-known olive-oil labels. This gave the Spanish company control of half the Italian market and made it the world's leader in olive-oil sales. Some people feared that smaller Italian brands would be forced to sell up as a result of this takeover.

▼ *A farmer checks his grapes at a vineyard in Tuscany, western Italy.*

IT'S A FACT!

Eight per cent of Italy's farmland is used to grow organic crops. Only Australia and Argentina devote a larger proportion of available farmland to organic farming.

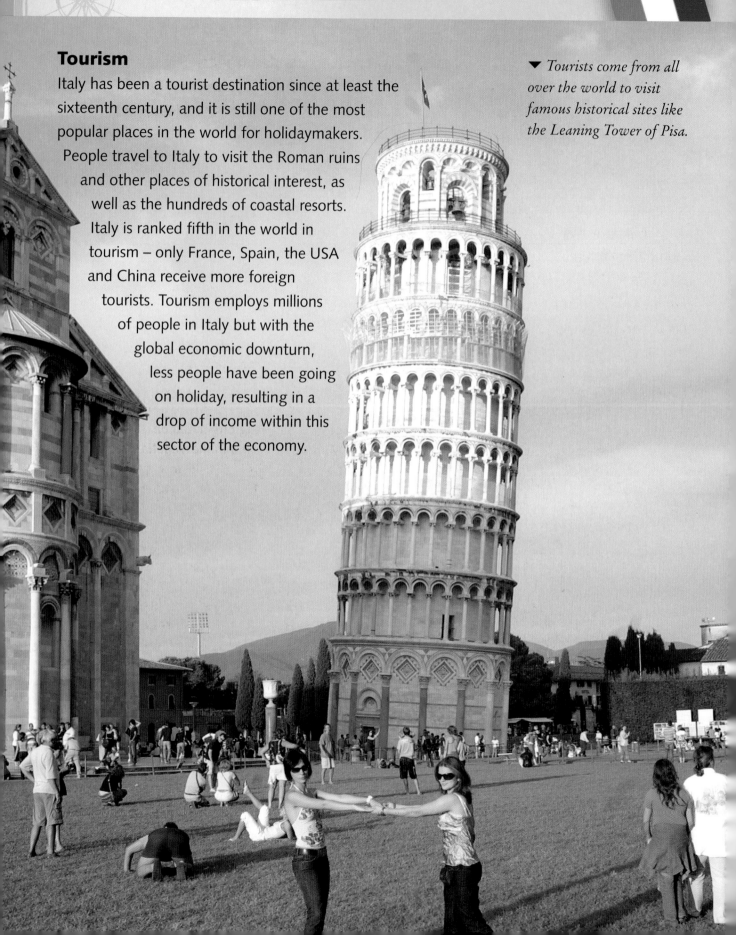

Tourism

Italy has been a tourist destination since at least the sixteenth century, and it is still one of the most popular places in the world for holidaymakers. People travel to Italy to visit the Roman ruins and other places of historical interest, as well as the hundreds of coastal resorts. Italy is ranked fifth in the world in tourism – only France, Spain, the USA and China receive more foreign tourists. Tourism employs millions of people in Italy but with the global economic downturn, less people have been going on holiday, resulting in a drop of income within this sector of the economy.

▼ *Tourists come from all over the world to visit famous historical sites like the Leaning Tower of Pisa.*

Cars

Many of the world's most prestigious (and expensive) sports cars are Italian, including Ferrari, Lamborghini, Maserati, Bugatti and De Tomaso. The motor-vehicle industry is important to the Italian economy, as cars are one of its biggest exports. The car manufacturer Fiat is the largest in Italy, and in 2009 it merged with the American car company Chrysler. It was hoped that this merger would create a bigger market for Italian cars in the USA.

▼ *Glass-blowing on the island of Murano in Venice. The craft has been practised here for centuries.*

Hand-made in Italy

Unlike China, where most goods are mass-produced in large factories, many Italian products are still custom-made by small, family-owned businesses. Clothing, ceramics and glassware are often produced in this way by skilled craftsmen, and exported all over the world.

IT STARTED HERE

Glass-blowing

Some of the world's finest glass comes from Italy, where the process of glass-blowing originated on Murano, an island in the Venetian lagoon. Venetian glass is now much sought-after. These unique items are beautiful – and expensive!

Government and politics

Italy is a republic, which means that it is not ruled by a king or queen, but by representatives elected by the Italian people. There are many political parties, and the government changes frequently.

Government organization

Until the end of World War II, Italy was ruled by a king. In 1946, the Italian people voted to abolish the monarchy and become a republic. The following year a constitution was established. Italy now has a president and a prime minister. Unlike the USA, where the president is the head of government, the president of Italy is only a ceremonial figure. The prime minister is the head of government and runs the country.

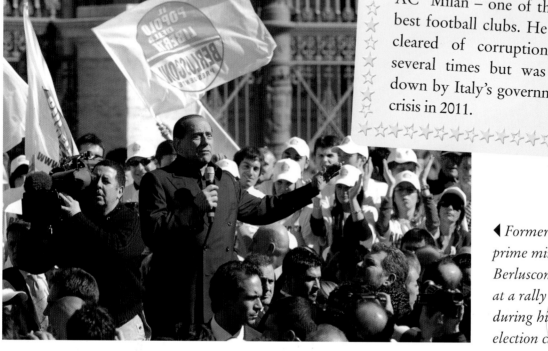

◀ *Former Italian prime minister Silvio Berlusconi speaks at a rally in Turin during his 2008 election campaign.*

Italy and the EU

Although Italy was one of the founders of the European Union, its relationship with other EU members has not always been good. In 2003, there were protests all over the country when Italy joined with the UK and Spain in supporting the US invasion of Iraq. Germany and France, traditionally allies of Italy, were against the invasion. In 2008, Italy rebelled against the EU's climate-change goals. The Italian prime minister argued that the plans were too expensive and that Italy could not afford to meet the goals. The following year, the prime minister threatened to veto the EU Energy and Climate Package.

IT'S A FACT!

Italy is among the worst-performing states in the Climate Change Performance Index, which ranks countries according to their emissions and how well they are meeting climate-change targets.

▼ *Italy chose to support the US-led invasion of Iraq in 2003. Italian troops remained in Iraq until 2006.*

▶ *Northern cities are filled with shops selling expensive designer items, and the people who live there have money to spend. In the south, it's a different story.*

North and South

The division of Italy into the more prosperous north and the poorer south is a source of tension within the country. Generally, Italians in the north of the country have a lot more money than those in the south. The gross domestic product per person is almost three times higher in the richest northern areas, such as Bologna and Milan, than in the south. Southern Italy includes eight regions with 35 per cent of the population, but is largely underdeveloped. Many of the people who live there have a hard life.

Women in Italy

In the 1970s, Italian women won the right to divorce their husbands, and in 2001 Italy had more female business managers and administrators than any other country.

IT'S A FACT!

Women make up only 21 per cent of the members of parliament in Italy, making it joint 51st (with China) in the world rankings. European nations such as Spain, Belgium and the Netherlands have percentages in the 30s. The top country, Rwanda, has 56 per cent women MPs.

Now, though, it seems that feminism is out of fashion. Italian television has been accused of promoting sexism, with game shows that feature attractive women in bikinis. Many people blame former prime minister, Silvio Berlusconi, for this trend because he owns the television networks. Italy also now has the lowest percentage of working women in Europe, and women hold only two per cent of top management positions.

The mafia

The mafia is a large criminal organization that is believed to have begun on the Italian island of Sicily in the late nineteenth century. The mafia controls many businesses and large farming operations, as well as the trade in illegal drugs. In the past, Italian politicians

GOING GLOBAL

Due to emigration from Italy in the late nineteenth and early twentieth centuries, there are now mafia groups in several countries, including the USA, Canada and Australia. Although these groups, or 'families', are usually independent of one another, they have similar structures and codes of conduct.

and judges have even been linked to the mafia. Although many mafia suspects have been arrested since the 1980s, the mafia is still big business in Italy, especially in the south, and mafia groups also exist in many other countries.

◀ *Mafia boss Bernardo Provenzano was arrested in 2006, but the organization continues in Italy and around the world.*

Italy in 2020

Although it is a relatively wealthy country by international standards, Italy faces several problems. These must be addressed in the next few years in order to improve the economy and the quality of life for the Italian people, particularly in the south.

Settling debts

Italy has one of the largest public debts in the world. This has put pressure on the economy, which may become worse in the future. It may be a particular problem for future generations if the population continues to age and there are fewer people working and paying taxes. The number of retired people compared to those in employment is on the rise. In 2011, 20 per cent of the population was 65 years or above and the country had one of the lowest birth rates in Europe. Unless there is a baby boom, the population will continue to age. To address this problem, Italy may have to encourage more immigrants to fill the labour gap.

GLOBAL LEADER

Healthcare

Italy has a national healthcare system similar to the National Health Service in the UK, in which healthcare is free to all Italian citizens. The World Health Organization recently rated Italy's healthcare system as the second best in the world, after France.

▼ *Italy needs a baby boom to address the problem of its ageing population.*

Getting ahead

To be elected to government in Italy, a person has to be at least 40 years old, and there is no maximum age. Because there are so many political parties, with all different ideas, it can be hard for young, educated Italians to get ahead if their politics are different from those of the people in power. More than half of all university graduates admitted they would like to work in a country where advancement is based on ability, not politics. The government may have to rethink such policies if it wants to encourage young people to stay in Italy.

▲ *These young people are earning money by busking in the street. It can be hard for young people to establish good careers in Italy.*

Environmental issues

By 2020, Italy will need to have seriously addressed its environmental problems. While many countries are reducing their greenhouse-gas emissions, Italy's have risen in the past 20 years. The goals set by the Kyoto Protocol may encourage Italy to work harder at reducing emissions and pollution. The country may also turn more to renewable energy sources to meet its needs. Italy is likely to double its capacity target for expanding the use of wind energy as it aims to meet EU goals for boosting renewable power.

IT'S A FACT!

Italy generated about 3.5 billion kilowatt hours of electricity on wind farms in 2006 – equal to about one per cent of total power demand. That's enough to meet the needs of over 4.5 million Italians.

Glossary

constitution a document that lays out the main laws of a nation. Laws are not allowed to be passed that contradict a country's constitution.

economy the financial system of a country or region, including how much money is made from the production and sale of goods and services.

emigration when someone leaves the country of their birth to settle in another country.

emissions gases that are given off during industrial processes or by vehicles.

ethnic group a group of people classed together according to their racial, national, linguistic or cultural origin or background.

export to send or transport products or materials abroad for sale or trade.

feminism a strong belief that women should have the same rights and opportunities as men.

glacier a large mass of ice that moves very slowly down a mountain valley.

gladiators men who entertained the public by fighting each other or wild animals in ancient Roman times.

global warming the gradual rise in temperatures on the surface of the Earth, caused by changes in the amount of greenhouse gases in the atmosphere.

greenhouse gas a gas that helps trap warmth in the atmosphere, which can contribute to global warming if too much is generated on Earth.

gross domestic product (GDP) the total amount of money a country earns every year.

immigrant a person who has moved to another country to live.

lagoon a large pool of seawater.

Muslim a follower of the Islamic religion.

peninsula a large mass of land that juts out into a body of water.

pollution spoiling the environment with man-made waste such as vehicle emissions, waste gases from factories, or chemicals from fertilizers.

population density the number of people living in a square kilometre or square mile of a country.

Renaissance a revival of learning and culture that began in Italy in the fourteenth century and lasted until the seventeenth century.

republic a system of government in which people elect officials to make decisions on their behalf, rather than being ruled by a king or queen.

rural relating to the countryside.

sexism a belief that people of the opposite sex are inferior.

veto to vote against something.

Further information

Books

Italy (Discover Countries)
by Kelly Davis
(Wayland, 2012)

Italy (Welcome to My Country)
by N. Frank and J. Sander Hausam
(Franklin Watts, 2007)

We're from Italy
by Vicky Parker
(Heinemann Library, 2006)

Italy (Letters from Around the World)
by Fiona Tankard
(Cherrytree Books, 2008)

Italy and the Italians
by E. Needham
(Franklin Watts, 2004)

Websites

www.italia.it/en/home.html
This is the official Italian tourist information site, with maps and information on Italy.

www.travelforkids.com/Funtodo/Italy/italy.htm
Take a journey through Italy with this fun site, travelling from Rome to Pompeii.

http://europa.eu/europago/welcome.jsp and http://europa.eu/youth
These European Union sites have been set up especially for children and young people.

http://kids.nationalgeographic.com/kids/places/find/italy/
This site has facts, photos, a map and a video about Italy.

http://www.socialstudiesforkids.com/subjects/economics.htm
Get to grips with economics with this site where topics such as money, trade and budgets are explained.

Every effort has been made by the publisher to ensure that these websites contain no inappropriate or offensive material. However, because of the nature of the Internet, it is impossible to guarantee that the content of these sites will not be altered. We strongly advise that Internet access is supervised by a responsible adult.

Index

Numbers in **bold** indicate pictures